DELAYED,
Not DENIED!

Books by Tim Barker

Anticipating the Return of Christ
At Your Feet
Called Camp 2025
Discovering God in the Secret Places
End Times
God's Revelation and Your Future
It's Not All About Sitting at the Head Table
Mighty Men of Courage from the Bible
Ministry Is Way Too Good Not to Enjoy It
My Jesus Journey
My Jesus Journey: Crescendo
My Jesus Journey: Glissando
My Jesus Journey: Rhapsody
Names of God
Open Doors
One Book of Jonah Is Enough
One. Less. Stone.
Our Privilege of Joy
Reflecting Christ Through the Fruit of the Spirit
The Age of Uncertainty
The Authentic Christian: Revealing Christ through the Fruit of the Spirit
The Call of Ephesians
The Lord with Us
The Night Heaven Broke Its Silence
The Twelve: Taking Up the Mantle of Christ
The Vision of Nehemiah: God's Plan for Righteous Living
Truth, Love & Redemption: The Holy Spirit for Today
Unified Church
Your Invitation to Christ

DELAYED,
Not DENIED!

Tim R. Barker, D. Min.

Network Pastor/Superintendent
South Texas Ministry Network

DELAYED, NOT DENIED

By Tim Barker

1st ed.

ISBN: 979-8-9959577-0-6

DEDICATION

To the ones who have whispered the same prayer more times than they can count…
Who have watched days turn into months, and months into years…
Wondering if heaven heard them at all—

This is for you.

For every quiet tear, every flicker of hope you refused to let die…
Every moment you chose to believe when disbelief would have been easier…
For the strength it took to keep asking, to keep trusting…
Even when the silence felt like an answer in itself.

May these pages remind you that waiting is not forgetting…
That unseen work is still work…

And that sometimes the longest-held prayers
are the ones held most carefully.

You are not alone in the waiting.

Tim R. Barker

PREFACE

What about when God doesn't answer?

When we rise from our knees and are bombarded with silence from heaven?

Too many pastors walk away from the pulpit because they think God no longer answers prayer.

The Word says God's silence has a purpose, and it's not His will for us to become frustrated and give up.

God wants to discover how much trust you have in Him.

Does He get the benefit of the doubt, or is our plan the only one we're willing to trust?

It's vital to remember the story of Daniel. Daniel's authenticity in God was already established. He had nothing to prove, not even to God.

Yet, for 21 days, Daniel's prayer went unanswered. Had God finally washed His hands of Daniel? Did He consider the prophet washed up and useless?

Was it time for Daniel to walk away?

The Word tells us the answer was already given ***even though it did not reach Daniel for three weeks.***

I want you to know that God still hears and answers prayer.

Never doubt. *Never get up from your knees with a question of your worth in God's eyes.*

He sees you.

He knows you.

And His answer is already on the way.

TABLE OF CONTENTS

INTRODUCTION

Delayed... But Never Denied

There is a moment every believer faces.

It is not the moment when God speaks.
And it is not the moment when breakthrough comes.

It is the moment in between.

The moment when:

- You prayed… but nothing changed
- You believed… but nothing moved
- You stood in faith… but nothing happened

And in that moment, the question begins to whisper:

“Did God really hear me?”

But what if the issue is not that God didn't answer…

What if the issue is that you don't yet understand the delay?

Because the truth is simple—but powerful:

Delayed does not mean denied.

In Daniel chapter 10, we are given a rare glimpse behind the curtain of the natural world into the reality of the Spirit.

Daniel prayed.

God answered immediately.

But the answer did not arrive when expected.

Why?

Because there was resistance.

And what Daniel experienced then…
Believers are still experiencing now.

This book exists to help you understand that space:

The space between:

- Promise and fulfillment

- Prayer and manifestation
- Faith and visible results

Because if you misunderstand delay…

You will walk away from what God already released.

But if you understand it…

You will endure it.

And if you endure it…

You will step into everything God has promised.

Because what God has spoken over your life…

Is not denied.

It may be delayed…

But it is not denied.

CHAPTER 1

THE SILENCE THAT TESTS YOUR FAITH

There is a kind of silence that is not empty—
It is holy.
It is the space where your faith is refined.
It is the moment between what God said… and what you see.

Every believer will face this silence.

Not because God has forgotten,
but because He is forming something deeper than answers—
He is forming trust.

WHEN HEAVEN SEEMS QUIET

- You prayed
- You believed
- You obeyed

And yet—**nothing moved.**

The silence feels heavy.

You question yourself:

- "Did I miss God?"
- "Did I pray wrong?"
- "Did He change His mind?"

But silence is not punishment.

It is an invitation.

God does some of His greatest work in the quiet—not when He is shouting, but when He is shaping our lives.

In Exodus 14, when Israel stood trapped between the Red Sea and Pharaoh's army…

God didn't speak immediately.

He let them feel the silence long enough…

for faith **to rise above fear**.

And then… He said, "Move forward."

SILENCE REVEALS MORE THAN YOU REALIZE

The waiting doesn't just expose the delay—**it exposes you**.

It reveals:

- What you really believe about God
- What you depend on for peace
- Whether your confidence rests in outcome or in presence

Because when the noise fades, **your foundation is revealed.**

- "Silence doesn't test your prayer—it tests your posture."
- "When you cannot hear God's voice, He is testing your trust in His nature."
- "Faith is not proven by what you hear—it is proven by what you hold onto when you don't."

GOD SPEAKS BEFORE HE GOES SILENT

Many times, divine silence follows a divine statement.
God says something—then steps back to see if you'll stand on it.

Think of Abraham.
God promised a son.
Then decades of silence.

Yet Abraham believed anyway.

The silence was not the absence of the promise—it was the environment in which **faith grew around it**.

If God spoke to you once,
you don't need Him to repeat Himself—
you need to remember what He said.

THE DISCIPLINE OF STILLNESS

Psalm 46:10 says,

"Be still, and know that I am God."

Stillness is not inactivity.

It is trust in motion.

It is choosing **rest** over **panic**,

faith over **fear**,

surrender over **striving**.

Stillness says: "I don't have to see movement to know He's moving."

Daniel understood this. Before the angel appeared, before an answer came…

He set his heart to seek God—

and stayed there.

- He didn't move
- He didn't waver
- He didn't rush

He let stillness become strength.

WHAT THE SILENCE PRODUCES

The silence you're enduring now
is producing something you'll need later.

It is building:

Depth – so your roots go deeper than emotion.
Discipline – so faith outlasts delay.
Discernment – so you hear beyond noise.
Dependency – so you learn God is enough.

You may not see progress…

But heaven is measuring growth differently.

You're not being ignored…

You're being equipped.

THE HIDDEN SIDE OF SILENCE

1 Kings 19 reveals Elijah in a cave, desperate to hear God.

There's wind… earthquake… fire.

But God is not in any of them.

Then—

A still, small voice.

That's where the power was.

Not in noise.
Not in spectacle.

In stillness.

That moment teaches us:

God is often most active when He feels most absent.

- "Silence is not empty—it is full of instruction."
- "The quiet is not God's withdrawal—it is His whisper."
- "You may not hear Him loudly, but you can trust that He's listening completely."

WHY GOD ALLOWS SILENT SEASONS

To Mature Your Faith – so you're guided by conviction, not confirmation.

To Clarify Your Motives – to remove any pursuit that's about outcome, not intimacy.

To Refine Your Hearing – to recognize His voice apart from emotion or noise.

To Prove His Word – to show that what He said still stands in silence.

God doesn't test you to fail you…

He tests you to prepare you.

WHAT TO DO IN THE SILENCE

When heaven is quiet:

- Keep praying — even when you feel nothing
- Keep believing — even when nothing looks different
- Keep worshiping — even when you don't understand

Because what you sustain in silence…

Positions you for what you'll carry in fulfillment.

Daniel did not stop seeking.

And on the twenty-first day, the silence broke.

THE TURNING POINT

There will come a day when what has been quiet suddenly speaks back.

The silence that stretched you **will make sense**.

You'll see that heaven was never ignoring you—

It was **preparing the answer to reach you**.

And when that moment comes, you'll thank God not only for the answer…

But for the silence that made you ready to receive it.

CLOSING DECLARATION

Speak this over your life:

- God is not absent in my silence
- Heaven heard me the first time I prayed
- I am being strengthened in the stillness
- My faith will endure until I hear again

CLOSING PRAYER

Father,

Teach us to trust You when You are quiet.

Remind us that silence is not distance.
Anchor our hearts when we cannot feel You.
Build our faith where sight has failed.

And in the stillness—

Let our confidence rest in who You are,

Not just in what You say.

In Jesus' name, Amen.

CHAPTER 2

WHEN HEAVEN SAYS YES FIRST

There is a truth that many believers struggle to grasp.

It is not that God is unwilling to answer.

It is not that God is unaware of your need.

And it is not that God is delaying because He is distant.

The truth is this:

God often answers before you ever see the answer.

And if you don't understand that…

You will misinterpret your entire situation.

DANIEL'S DEFINING MOMENT

In **Daniel 10**, we are given one of the clearest revelations in all of Scripture about how heaven responds to prayer.

Daniel has been fasting and praying for 21 days.

- No response
- *No vision*
- No breakthrough

Just silence.

And then—suddenly—the answer arrives.

And the angel says something that should reshape the way we think about prayer forever:

"From the first day that you set your heart to understand… your words were heard…"

Let that settle in your spirit.

From the first day.

Not the twenty-first day.
Not when the angel arrived.
Not when Daniel felt something.

Day one.

HEAVEN DOES NOT HESITATE

We often think of God as if He is slow to respond.

As if He needs to:

- Think about it
- Consider it
- Decide whether or not He wants to move

But Scripture paints a completely different picture.

Jesus said in **Matthew 7:7**:

"Ask, and it will be given to you…"

And in **1 John 5:14**:

"If we ask anything according to His will… He hears us."

Not eventually.

Not after delay.

He hears immediately.

THE PROBLEM IS NOT IN HEAVEN

So, if heaven responds immediately…

Why does earth experience delay?

The Book of Daniel gives us the answer:

"But the prince of Persia withstood me…"

The issue was not God's response.

The issue was resistance between heaven and earth.

THERE IS A SPACE BETWEEN

This is the part we don't often talk about.

There is a space between:

- Heaven releasing the answer
- And you receiving the answer

And that space is not empty.

It is active.

It is contested.

It is spiritual.

Paul explains it this way:

Ephesians 6:12 …

"We wrestle not against flesh and blood…"

Which means:

Not everything you experience is natural.

Some things are spiritual.

A NEW UNDERSTANDING OF DELAY

Let me say this clearly:

Delay is not always about God.

Sometimes…

Delay is about what is happening *between* God's answer and your reality.

ILLUSTRATION: THE SHIPMENT

Think about it like this.

You order something online.

The moment you click "purchase"—the order is confirmed.

It is processed immediately.

But you don't receive it immediately.

Why?

Because there is a journey between confirmation and arrival.

Now hear this spiritually:

Your prayer was **confirmed in heaven**…

But it is still **in transit in the Spirit**.

- “Answered in heaven does not always mean received on earth—yet.”
- “Just because it hasn’t arrived doesn’t mean it hasn’t been released.”
- “God is not late—your answer is in transit.”

WHY THIS CHANGES EVERYTHING

If you misunderstand this…

You will assume:

- God is ignoring you
- God is delaying you
- God is withholding from you

But when you understand this…

You realize:

God already said yes.

And that changes how you pray.

YOU STOP BEGGING AND START BELIEVING

When Daniel didn't see an answer immediately…

He didn't stop praying.

He didn't assume God said no.

He stayed in position.

Because something in him knew:

"If I seek God… God responds."

JESUS TAUGHT THIS PATTERN

In **Luke 18**, Jesus tells the story of a persistent widow.

And He concludes with this statement:

"Men ought always to pray and not lose heart."

Why?

Because persistence is not about convincing God…

It's about **standing in faith until manifestation comes**.

APPLICATION: WHERE ARE YOU RIGHT NOW?

Let's bring this into your life.

Where are you waiting?

- A prayer you prayed months ago
- A promise you're still believing for
- A breakthrough you haven't seen yet

And the question is not:

"Has God answered?"

The real question is:

"Do you believe He answered already?"

YOUR BELIEF DETERMINES YOUR POSTURE

If you think God hasn't answered…

You will:

- Grow frustrated
- Lose confidence
- Pull back in faith

But if you believe God answered on **Day One**…

You will:

- Stand firm
- Stay consistent
- Keep expecting

FAITH LIVES IN THE GAP

Faith is not just believing God *will* do something.

Faith is believing God **has already moved**…

Even when you haven't seen it yet.

HEBREWS SAYS IT BEST

Hebrews 11:1 is a much-loved verse:

"Faith is the substance of things hoped for… the evidence of things not seen."

Faith is the evidence…

Before the evidence appears.

- "Faith doesn't wait for evidence—it becomes the evidence."
- "You don't need to see it to believe it—you need to believe it to see it."
- "God's answer is not determined by your timeline."

THE DANGER OF WALKING AWAY TOO EARLY

Many believers quit in the gap.

They stop praying.

They stop believing.

They stop expecting.

Not because God didn't answer…

But because they didn't understand the delay.

And this is the tragedy.

They walk away…

From what was already on the way.

FINAL THOUGHT

Daniel didn't receive his answer on Day One.

But it was released on Day One.

And if he had stopped praying…

He would never have seen what had already been sent.

CLOSING DECLARATION

Let this settle in your spirit:

- Heaven heard me immediately
- God responded instantly
- My answer was released on Day One
- And I will not quit before it arrives

CLOSING PRAYER

Father,

Help us to trust what we cannot see.
Help us to believe what You have already done.
Strengthen us in the waiting…
And anchor us in faith.

Teach us to stand…

Until what You released in heaven…

Arrives in our lives.

In Jesus' name, Amen.

CHAPTER 3

THE WAR OVER YOUR ANSWER

There are some truths that, once you see them, you cannot unsee them.

This is one of them:

Not every delay is passive.
Some delays are contested.

There are moments in your life when what you are waiting on is not simply “taking time”…

God has not put the brakes on your answer. *He’s not testing you.* He’s already released it to you.

Rather, it is being **fought over**.

DANIEL PULLED BACK THE CURTAIN

Daniel chapter 10 gives us one of the clearest revelations in all of Scripture about spiritual conflict.

Daniel prayed.

God answered immediately.

But the answer did not arrive when expected.

Why?

Because the angel said:

"The prince of Persia withstood me..."

Let that settle in your spirit.

The answer wasn't delayed because God hesitated.

The answer was delayed because it was **resisted**.

THERE IS A WAR YOU CANNOT SEE

One of the greatest deceptions of the enemy...

Is convincing believers that everything is natural.

That every struggle is:

- Circumstantial
- Emotional
- Physical

But Scripture reveals something deeper.

Ephesians 6:12 says,

“We wrestle not against flesh and blood, but against principalities… powers… rulers of darkness…”

Which means:

There are battles happening…

That you cannot see with your natural eyes.

YOUR LIFE HAS MORE SIGNIFICANCE THAN YOU THINK

If there is warfare over your answer…

That means your answer matters.

Let me say it plainly:

The enemy does not fight what is insignificant.

He doesn't resist what is irrelevant.

He doesn't oppose what carries no impact.

- "If it's being resisted, it's because it's valuable."
- "The level of opposition often reveals the weight of your assignment."
- "Hell does not waste energy on things that don't matter."

THIS WAS NOT ABOUT DANIEL ALONE

This is critical to understand.

Daniel was not just praying for himself.

He was praying about:

- His people
- His nation
- God's prophetic plan

Which means:

The answer he was waiting for had **larger implications**.

And so does yours.

Some of what you're praying for is not just about you.

It's about:

- Your family
- Your future
- Your influence
- Your assignment

And that's why there is resistance.

THE ENEMY'S OBJECTIVE

The enemy has one primary strategy when it comes to delay:

Interrupt the process long enough for you to give up.

Because he knows something you often forget:

If you **stay in faith long enough**…

You will see what God promised.

So he applies pressure.

Not to destroy you immediately…

But to wear you down gradually.

To weaken your faith.

To make you question:

- “Is this worth it?”
- “Is this really going to happen?”
- “Did God really say that?”

Sound familiar?

That’s the same strategy from the beginning.

In Genesis 3, the serpent asked:

“Did God really say…?”

Because if he can get you to question the Word…

He can weaken your faith.

THE BATTLEFIELD IS YOUR MIND

The war over your answer is not just happening in the Spirit…

It is also happening in your thinking.

That’s why **2 Corinthians 10:4–5** says:

“We cast down arguments… and every high thing that exalts itself against the knowledge of God…”

Because the enemy knows:

If he can win your thoughts…

He can influence your response.

- “The battle is not just around you—it is within you.”
- “If the enemy can control your thoughts, he can weaken your faith.”
- “What you believe in the delay determines whether you endure it.”

WHY THE DELAY FEELS SO HEAVY

Have you ever noticed that delay doesn’t just feel like time passing?

It feels like pressure.

That’s because it is.

You are not just waiting…

You are **standing under resistance**.

Daniel felt it too.

Daniel described himself as being in mourning for 21 days.

This wasn’t casual waiting.

This was heavy.

Burdened.

Intense.

AND yet—he stayed.

This is what sets Daniel apart.

He didn't stop praying.

He didn't quit seeking.

He didn't walk away.

He stayed in position…

Until breakthrough came.

This is where many people lose.

Not because God didn't answer.

But because they stopped before it arrived.

JESUS warned us about this.

In **Luke 18**, Jesus tells the story of a persistent widow, and He ends with this:

"Men ought always to pray and not lose heart."

Why?

Because losing heart is the enemy's goal.

THE WAR IS NOT JUST OVER YOUR ANSWER

It's over your **endurance**.

Because if you endure…

You win.

James confirms it.

James 1:12 says,

"Blessed is the one who endures… for when he has been approved, he will receive…"

Notice that *endurance* comes before *receiving.*

- "The promise is not given to the quickest—it is given to the one who endures."
- "Breakthrough is not about speed—it is about staying."
- "If you don't quit, you don't lose."

HEAVEN HAS ALREADY ENGAGED

Now here is what you must understand.

If there is war over your answer…

That means heaven is already involved.

Daniel's answer didn't originate on earth.

It originated in heaven.

And once heaven released it…

The battle began.

Which means this:

You are not trying to get God to move.

God has already moved.

You are standing in the reality of what God has already released.

THIS CHANGES YOUR POSTURE

You don't pray from desperation…

You pray from **confidence**.

You don't beg…

You believe.

FINAL DECLARATION

Let this settle deep in your spirit:

- There is a war over what belongs to me
- But God has already released the answer
- Heaven is already engaged
- And I will not quit in the middle of the battle

CLOSING THOUGHT

The war is real.

The resistance is real.

The delay is real.

But so is the promise.

And the same God who released the answer…

Will ensure it arrives.

CLOSING PRAYER

Father,

Open our eyes to what we cannot see.
Strengthen us in the middle of the battle.
Guard our minds, anchor our faith, and steady our hearts.

Help us to stand…
Even when we feel pressure…
Even when we feel resistance…
Even when we feel delay.

And let us see what You have already released.

In Jesus' name, Amen.

CHAPTER 4

SPIRITUAL RESISTANCE IS REAL

There is a mistake many believers make.

They believe in God.
They believe in prayer.
They believe in promises.

But they struggle to believe in resistance.

Not intellectually…

But practically.

WE BELIEVE IN VICTORY… BUT FORGET THE BATTLE

We love to quote victory Scriptures:

- “We are more than conquerors…” (Romans 8:37)
- “No weapon formed against me shall prosper…” (Isaiah 54:17)
- “The Lord will fight for you…” (Exodus 14:14)

And all of that is true.

But here’s the part we often overlook:

If there were no battle… there would be no need for victory.

DANIEL SHOWS US WHAT WE DON’T NORMALLY SEE

Daniel didn’t just experience delay.

He was shown *why* the delay happened.

There was resistance.

There was opposition.

There was conflict in the unseen realm.

And that revelation forces us to confront something:

Spiritual resistance is not rare. It is normal.

JESUS FACED IT—WHY WOULDN'T WE?

If anyone ever walked in perfect alignment with God, it was Jesus.

And yet…

- He was tempted in the wilderness (Matthew 4)
- He was opposed in ministry (Mark 3:22)
- He was resisted by religious systems (John 5:16)
- He was attacked spiritually before the cross (Luke 22:44)

So, if Jesus faced resistance…

Why would we assume we won't?

RESISTANCE DOESN'T ALWAYS LOOK LIKE A BATTLE

This is where we need clarity.

Spiritual resistance doesn't always show up as something dramatic.

It often looks subtle.

Quiet and normal.

HOW RESISTANCE SHOWS UP IN REAL LIFE

Let's bring this into everyday experience.

Spiritual resistance often looks like:

1. Unusual Frustration

Things that should be simple… feel difficult.

Doors that should open… don't.
Progress that should happen… stalls.

2. Persistent Discouragement

You're doing the right thing…

But you feel like quitting.

3. Mental Pressure

Your thoughts become:

- Negative
- *Doubtful*
- Overwhelming

4. Loss of Momentum

You were moving forward…

But suddenly everything slows down.

5. Increased Opposition

Conflict increases.
Resistance rises.
Things get harder—not easier.

AND HERE'S THE DANGER

If you don't recognize resistance…

You will misinterpret your situation.

You will think:

- "Something is wrong with me"
- "God must not be in this"
- "Maybe I should stop"

Instead, consider this:

- "What you misinterpret, you will mishandle."
- "If you don't recognize resistance, you will retreat from your assignment."
- "Not every closed door is rejection—some are opposition."

RESISTANCE OFTEN APPEARS AT THE POINT OF BREAKTHROUGH

One of the most important patterns in Scripture is this:

Resistance intensifies **right before receiving a breakthrough in your spirit... right before God's answer reaches you**.

Exodus 14 shows us the pattern:

Israel is leaving Egypt.

They are finally free.

And suddenly—

Pharaoh's army is behind them.
The Red Sea is in front of them.

Resistance increased…

Right before deliverance.

1 Kings 18 becomes a victory dance:

Elijah prays for rain.

Nothing happens.

He prays again.

Still nothing.

But on the seventh time…

A cloud appears.

THIS IS A PATTERN

Pressure rises…

Before things shift.

- “The pressure you feel may be proof that breakthrough is near.”
- “Resistance often increases when you’re closest to the answer.”
- “The enemy fights hardest at the edge of your breakthrough.”

The enemy wants you to misread the moment.

If he can convince you that resistance means “stop”…

You will walk away at the worst possible time.

BUT WHAT IF RESISTANCE MEANS ‘KEEP GOING’?

What if:

- The frustration is not failure
- The pressure is not punishment
- The delay is not denial

What if it’s confirmation…

That you are on the right path?

PAUL EXPERIENCED THIS TOO

In **1 Corinthians 16:9**, Paul says:

“A great and effective door has opened to me… and there are many adversaries.”

Notice what Paul says:

Opportunity and opposition…

Showed up at the same time.

That changes how you see your situation.

Opposition doesn’t always mean:

“You missed God”

Sometimes it means:

“You found the right door”

RESISTANCE IS NOT GREATER THAN GOD

Let’s be clear.

Spiritual resistance is real…

But it is not ultimate.

God is still sovereign.

God is still in control.

God is still working.

Isaiah 59:19 says:

"When the enemy comes in like a flood, the Spirit of the Lord will lift up a standard..."

Romans 8:31 tells us:

"If God is for us, who can be against us?"

- "Resistance may be real—but it is never greater than God."
- "The presence of opposition does not cancel the promise."
- "God's purpose is stronger than any resistance you face."

WHAT DO YOU DO WHEN YOU FEEL RESISTANCE?

This is where it becomes practical.

When you recognize resistance, you don't:

- Panic
- Quit
- Pull back

You do what Daniel did.

You stay in position.

You keep:

- Praying
- *Believing*
- Standing

Because your posture determines your outcome.

EPHESIANS GIVES US THE STRATEGY

Ephesians 6:13 says:

"Having done all… stand."

Not run.
Not retreat.

Stand.

- "Standing is a spiritual act of defiance against resistance."
- "You don't overcome by quitting—you overcome by staying."
- "Your breakthrough is often on the other side of your decision to stand."

FINAL APPLICATION

Let me ask you something:

Where are you experiencing resistance right now?

- In your family?
- In your faith?
- In your calling?
- In your future?

What if that resistance…

Is not a sign to stop…

But a sign to press in?

CLOSING DECLARATION

Say this over your life:

- I will not misinterpret resistance
- I will not quit under pressure
- I will not retreat from what God promised
- I will stand until I see breakthrough

CLOSING THOUGHT

Spiritual resistance is real…

But so is the power of God.

And the same God who allows you to face resistance…

Also gives you the strength to overcome it.

CLOSING PRAYER

Father,

Give us discernment to recognize resistance.
Give us strength to stand in the middle of it.
And give us faith to believe that You are working even now.

Help us not to quit…
Not to retreat…
Not to give up.

But to stand firm…

Until we see everything You have promised.

In Jesus' name, Amen.

CHAPTER 5

THE STRATEGY OF WEARINESS

Not every battle is loud.

Not every attack is obvious.

Some of the most dangerous moments in your life…

Will not come through crisis…

They will come through **fatigue**.

THE ENEMY DOESN'T ALWAYS FIGHT TO DESTROY YOU

Sometimes…

He fights to **drain you**.

Because if he can't stop God's promise…

He will try to stop your **endurance**.

WEARINESS IS SUBTLE— BUT STRATEGIC

You don't wake up one day and decide:

"I'm done."

It happens gradually.

Quietly.

Over time.

You get tired of:

- Waiting
- Praying
- Believing
- Hoping

And before you know it…

You're not standing in faith anymore—

You get up in the morning, look into the mirror, and realize you're tired.

Suddenly, you're just trying to ***survive the day***.

GALATIANS GIVES US THE WARNING

Galatians 6:9 says:

“Let us not grow weary in well doing, for in due season we shall reap—if we do not lose heart.”

That verse reveals something critical:

The promise is not the problem.
The process is not the problem.

Weariness is the threat.

THE ENEMY’S GOAL IS NOT ALWAYS IMMEDIATE FAILURE

His goal is to foster gradual disengagement from your faith in God.

He doesn’t need you to collapse publicly…

If he can get you to withdraw privately.

- “The enemy doesn’t have to destroy you if he can exhaust you.”
- “Weariness is the slow erosion of faith.”
- “You don’t lose all at once—you lose little by little.”

EVEN STRONG PEOPLE GET WEARY

This is important.

Weariness is not a sign of weakness.

It's a sign you've been **in the fight**.

1 Kings 19 paints this picture:

Elijah calls down fire from heaven.

He defeats the prophets of Baal.

It is one of the greatest moments of spiritual victory in Scripture.

And immediately after…

He runs.

He hides.

And he says:

"It is enough… take my life."

What happened?

He wasn't defeated.

He was **exhausted**.

VICTORY DOES NOT MAKE YOU IMMUNE TO WEARINESS

Sometimes the greatest attacks come:

After your biggest victories.
After your most intense seasons.
After you've poured out everything.

Because you are depleted.

And when you are depleted…

You are vulnerable.

WEARINESS AFFECTS HOW YOU SEE EVERYTHING

When you're tired…

- Problems look bigger
- God feels distant
- Hope feels fragile

The danger is perception.

Weariness doesn't just affect your strength—

It affects your **perspective**.

- "When you are weary, everything feels heavier than it actually is."

- "Exhaustion distorts reality."
- "What feels impossible may simply be what feels overwhelming."

Jesus addressed this directly.

In **Luke 18:1**, Jesus said:

"Men ought always to pray and not lose heart."

That phrase—"lose heart"—means:

To give up internally…
To grow faint in spirit…
To become discouraged…

THIS IS THE REAL BATTLE

The enemy is not just after your actions—

He's after your **heart**.

Because if you lose heart…

You will eventually lose position.

Daniel didn't just face resistance—he faced time.

Daniel prayed for 21 days.

Think about three weeks with heaven sealed against you, with your need pressing in on you.

That means:

21 days with no visible answer…
21 days of consistency…
21 days of pressing through silence…

That takes endurance.

Not just faith.

Endurance.

And that's what the enemy targets.

Not just your belief—

Your ability to **sustain belief over time**.

HEBREWS SPEAKS TO THIS

Hebrews 10:36 says:

"You have need of endurance…"

Because endurance is what carries you…

From promise to fulfillment…

What enables you to move from your knees to trust in the answer you desire from a caring and loving God.

Endurance comes *from and through our faith*.

The difference between those who receive and those who don't…

Is not always faith at the beginning.

It's **endurance in the middle**.

- "Anyone can start in faith—few know how to stay in it."
- "Endurance is faith stretched over time."
- "Breakthrough belongs to those who outlast the battle."

HOW WEARINESS SHOWS UP

Let's get practical.

Weariness doesn't always say:

"I quit."

It sounds like:

- "What's the point?"
- "Maybe this isn't going to happen."
- "I'm tired of trying."
- "I'll just settle."

And this is dangerous.

Because settling is not surrender to God…

It's surrender to pressure.

GOD'S ANSWER TO WEARINESS

God does not ignore weariness.

He addresses it.

Isaiah 40:29–31 is our source of strength:

"He gives power to the weak… Those who wait on the Lord shall renew their strength…"

RENEWAL IS AVAILABLE

God doesn't just command you to endure—

He empowers you to endure.

But there's a condition:

"Those who wait on the Lord…"

That means:

> Stay connected…
> Stay dependent…
> Stay engaged…

You don't overcome weariness by walking away.

You overcome weariness by:

Drawing closer

Jesus modeled this.

When Jesus was under pressure…

He withdrew to pray.

Not to escape—

But to be **refilled**.

- "You don't overcome exhaustion by disengaging—you overcome it by reconnecting."
- "The answer to weariness is not distance from God—it is deeper dependence on Him."
- "You are not running out—you are being called back in."

A WORD FOR THE WEARY

Let me speak directly to you:

If you're tired…

If you feel drained…

If you've been carrying more than you thought you could…

You are not failing.

You are fighting.

And God sees it.

He sees:

- Every prayer
- Every tear
- Every moment you didn't quit

Galatians 6:9 still stands:

"You will reap… if you do not lose heart."

That means:

> The harvest is not in question.
> The promise is not in doubt.

The only issue is—will you stay?

FINAL APPLICATION

Where are you weary right now?

- In your faith?
- In your calling?
- In your waiting?

And what would it look like…

If you got up from your knees and decided…

To **not quit today**?

CLOSING DECLARATION

Say this over your life:

- I will not lose heart
- I will not give in to weariness
- I will not abandon what God promised
- I will endure until I see it

CLOSING THOUGHT

Weariness is real… but it does not have the final word.

Because the same God who called you… Will sustain you.

CLOSING PRAYER

Father,

Strengthen every weary heart.
Restore every tired soul.
Renew our faith and steady our steps.

Help us to endure…
Help us to stand…
Help us to keep going…

Until we see everything You have promised.

In Jesus' name, Amen.

CHAPTER 6

DEVELOPMENT BEFORE DELIVERY

There is a truth about God that many people don't fully understand:

God is more committed to who you are becoming… than what you are receiving.

We often focus on:

- The answer
- The breakthrough
- The outcome

But God is focused on:

- The person
- The character
- The capacity

WE WANT DELIVERY—GOD PRIORITIZES DEVELOPMENT

We pray for:

- Open doors
- Favor
- Increase
- Opportunity

And God hears us.

But before He releases what we're asking for…

He begins working on who we are.

Because what you receive must be sustained.

If God gives you something…

That your character cannot handle…

What was meant to bless you…

Can overwhelm you.

- "God prepares the person before He releases the promise."
- "If you receive before you're ready, you may lose what you were given."

- “Delay is often God’s way of building capacity.”

DANIEL WAS ALREADY A MAN OF CHARACTER

By the time we reach Daniel 10…

Daniel is not a beginner.

He has already:

- Survived Babylon
- Remained faithful in exile
- Interpreted dreams
- Refused compromise

And yet—he is still being formed.

Even at this stage of his life…

God is still developing him.

Because development is not a season—

It is a lifestyle.

GOD NEVER STOPS FORMING YOU

The moment you stop growing…

You limit what God can do through you.

Romans explains the process.

Romans 5:3–4 says:

"Tribulation produces perseverance…
perseverance produces character…
and character produces hope."

Notice the order.

- Pressure…
- Produces perseverance…
- Which produces character…
- Which produces hope

WHAT YOU'RE GOING THROUGH HAS PURPOSE

The pressure you feel…

Is not random.

It is producing something.

James confirms it.

James 1:3–4 says:

"The testing of your faith produces patience…
that you may be complete…"

God is not trying to hurt you.

He is trying to **complete you**.

- "God is not punishing you—He is preparing you."
- "The process you're in is producing the person you need to become."
- "You are not stuck—you are being shaped."

BIBLICAL PATTERN: DEVELOPMENT ALWAYS COMES FIRST

Throughout Scripture, we see this pattern again and again.

Joseph

He had a dream.

But before the palace…

There was a pit.

Before leadership…

There was slavery.

Before promotion…

There was prison.

Why?

Because the dream required a man…

Who had been developed.

David

He was anointed king.

But he didn't sit on the throne immediately.

He went back to the field.

He faced lions and bears.

He endured rejection.

Why?

Because the crown required capacity.

Jesus

Even Jesus…

Spent 30 years in preparation…

Before 3 years of public ministry.

Let that sink in.

Preparation often takes longer…

Than manifestation.

And that's not a problem—it's a pattern.

We often mislabel the season.

We call it:

- Delay
- Waiting
- Nothing happening

But God calls it **development.**

- "What feels like delay may actually be development."
- "God is not wasting time—He is investing in you."
- "The hidden season is where strength is built."

DEVELOPMENT BUILDS CAPACITY

Let's talk about capacity.

Capacity is your ability to:

- Handle what God gives
- Carry what God releases
- Sustain what God builds

Without capacity—blessing becomes burden.

If your capacity is small…

Even a big blessing will feel overwhelming.

So God expands you first.

He stretches:

- Your patience
- Your faith
- Your endurance
- Your trust

And stretching is uncomfortable.

Growth rarely feels good in the moment.

It feels:

- Tight
- Pressured
- Challenging

But it is necessary.

Because where you are going…

Requires more than where you are.

- "God stretches you before He expands you."
- "The pressure you feel is the expansion you need."
- "You are being prepared for something bigger than you."

DEVELOPMENT ALSO BUILDS DEPENDENCE

One of the greatest things God does in development…

Is teach you to depend on Him.

Because success without dependence is dangerous.

If you reach a place where:

- You don't pray
- You don't seek
- You don't rely on God

Then success becomes your greatest vulnerability.

So God keeps you close.

Through the process.

Through the pressure.

Through the waiting.

So you learn this truth.

"I cannot do this without Him."

FINAL APPLICATION

Let me ask you:

What if this season is not about what you're waiting for…

But who you're becoming?

What if:

- The delay has purpose
- The pressure has meaning
- The waiting has value

What if you're being prepared?

Prepared for:

- Greater influence
- Greater responsibility
- Greater impact

CLOSING DECLARATION

Say this over your life:

- God is developing me
- God is increasing my capacity
- God is preparing me for what's next
- And I will be ready when it arrives

CLOSING THOUGHT

God is not just working on your situation.

He is working on you.

And when the time comes…

You won't just receive the promise—

You will be ready to carry it.

CLOSING PRAYER

Father,

Thank You for the work You are doing in us.
Even when we don't understand it…
Even when it feels difficult…

Shape us.
Strengthen us.
Prepare us.

Make us ready for everything You have prepared.

In Jesus' name, Amen.

CHAPTER 7

BUILT IN THE WAITING

Waiting is one of the most misunderstood seasons in the life of a believer.

We often see waiting as:

- Passive
- Unproductive
- Frustrating

But in the Kingdom of God…

Waiting is never wasted.

WAITING IS NOT EMPTY—IT IS CONSTRUCTIVE

You may feel like nothing is happening.

But spiritually…

Something is being built.

GOD BUILDS IN HIDDEN PLACES

The most significant work God does in your life…

Rarely happens in public.

It happens:

- In quiet moments
- *In unseen seasons*
- In places where no one is watching

Because God is not performing…

He is forming.

He is not trying to impress people…

He is trying to prepare you.

- "God builds in private what He intends to reveal in public."
- "The hidden season is where true strength is formed."
- "If you rush what God is building, you weaken what He wants to establish."

We can read in Isaiah where **God gives us the blueprint.**

Isaiah 40:31 says:

“Those who wait on the Lord shall renew their strength…”

Let’s pause there.

Waiting is not inactivity. It’s not getting up from your knees and binge-watching your favorite Christian comedian until God sends your answer.

It is an **exchange**.

WAITING IS WHERE STRENGTH IS RENEWED

You bring:

- Your weakness
- Your fatigue
- Your uncertainty

And God gives:

- Strength
- Stability
- Clarity

That means waiting is productive.

Even when it doesn’t feel like it.

DANIEL WAS BEING STRENGTHENED

During those 21 days…

Daniel wasn't just waiting.

He was:

- Fasting
- Seeking
- Positioning himself before God

And something was happening inside him.

Even before the answer arrived…

Daniel was being strengthened to receive it.

Because what God was about to reveal… required strength.

When the angel finally appears…

Daniel falls, weakened from his prayers.

He has to be touched and strengthened multiple times.

Why?

Because revelation requires capacity.

And waiting builds that capacity.

WAITING BUILDS IDENTITY

One of the greatest things formed in the waiting…

Is your identity.

Who are you when nothing is happening?

That question matters.

Because:

- It's easy to trust God when things are moving
- It's easy to believe when things are visible

But who are you…

When it's quiet?

That's where identity is tested.

Are you:

- Still faithful?
- Still committed?
- Still trusting?

Then God is preparing you.

- “Waiting reveals who you are when nothing is happening.”
- “Your identity is not proven in movement—it is proven in stillness.”
- “Who you are in the silence determines what you can handle in the spotlight.”

WAITING BUILDS DISCIPLINE

Let’s talk about discipline.

Because waiting requires:

- Consistency
- Persistence
- Stability

You don’t feel like it—but you do it anyway.

You pray… even when you don’t feel it.
You believe… even when you don’t see it.
You stay… even when you want to leave.

That builds spiritual muscle.

And muscle is built through resistance.

So the waiting is working on you.

Every day that you don’t quit…

You’re getting stronger.

WAITING BUILDS TRUST

Trust is not built when everything makes sense.

Trust is built when nothing does.

Proverbs 3:5–6 gives us reassurance:

"Trust in the Lord with all your heart…
and lean not on your own understanding…"

That's the challenge of waiting.

Because waiting often doesn't make sense.

And yet—you choose to trust.

Not because you understand…

But because you believe.

- "Trust is built in the absence of answers."
- "You don't trust God because you understand—you trust Him because He is faithful."
- "Waiting is where trust becomes real."

Waiting also builds intimacy.

Let's go deeper.

One of the most overlooked benefits of waiting…

Is intimacy with God.

Because when nothing else is moving…

You learn to sit with Him.

To seek Him.

To listen.

Not for what He can do…

But for who He is.

This is where relationship deepens.

Because you're no longer driven by outcome…

You're anchored in connection.

Psalm 27:14 is our hope in faith:

"Wait on the Lord… be of good courage… and He shall strengthen your heart."

WAITING STRENGTHENS THE HEART

Not just your situation.

Your heart.

And that changes everything.

Because when your heart is strong…

You can handle anything.

THE DANGER OF ESCAPING THE WAITING SEASON

Many people try to escape waiting.

They:

- Rush decisions
- Force outcomes
- Settle prematurely

But when you rush… you risk what God is building.

Because you step into something…

Before you're ready for it.

- "What you rush, you risk."
- "Premature movement can undo what God is trying to build."
- "Don't trade long-term strength for short-term relief."

God knows when you're ready.

God is not withholding from you.

He is waiting for the right moment—

When:

- You are ready
- The timing is right
- The foundation is secure

Ecclesiastes 3:1 gives us this:

"To everything there is a season…"

And God doesn't miss seasons.

He doesn't release too early.

He doesn't release too late.

FINAL APPLICATION

Let me ask you:

What if this waiting season…

Is the most important season of your life?

What if:

- Your strength is being built
- Your identity is being formed
- Your trust is being deepened

- Your relationship with God is being strengthened

What if this is preparation—not punishment?

CLOSING DECLARATION

Say this over your life:

- God is building me in this season
- My strength is increasing
- My faith is growing
- My foundation is being established
- And I will not rush what God is building

CLOSING THOUGHT

Waiting is not wasted.

It is where God builds the version of you…

That can carry what He has prepared.

CLOSING PRAYER

Father,

Thank You for what You are building in us.
Even in the waiting…
Even in the silence…

Strengthen us.
Stabilize us.
Deepen us.

Help us to trust the process…

And become everything You've called us to be.

In Jesus' name, Amen.

CHAPTER 8

FAITH THAT OUTLASTS DELAY

There is a difference between starting in faith…

…and **staying in faith**.

Most people don't struggle with believing God at the beginning.

They struggle with believing God…

Over time.

FAITH IS EASY WHEN IT'S FRESH

When God first speaks:

- Faith is strong
- Hope is high
- Expectation is clear

You feel it.

You believe it.

You're confident.

But time tests what emotion started.

Because eventually…

Time passes.

And nothing changes.

And that's where faith shifts from:
Emotion…
To endurance…

Hebrews defines real faith.

Hebrews 11:1 says:

"Faith is the substance of things hoped for, the evidence of things not seen."

Let's break that down.

Faith is:

- Substance
- Evidence

BEFORE YOU SEE ANYTHING

That means:

Faith doesn't come after proof…

Faith exists **before proof**.

Faith lives in the gap.

Between:

- What God said
- And what you see

And that gap can feel long.

Long enough to:

- Question
- Doubt
- Reconsider

But this is where faith becomes real.

Because real faith is not:

> "I believe because I see."

It is:

> "I believe even though I don't see."

QUOTABLE TRUTH

- “Faith is not sustained by sight—it is sustained by conviction.”
- “You don’t need evidence to believe—you need belief to see the evidence.”
- “Faith doesn’t wait for confirmation—it stands on the Word.”

ABRAHAM: THE MODEL OF ENDURING FAITH

Let’s look at Abraham.

God promised him a son.

But the promise didn’t happen immediately.

Years passed.

Then more years.

Then decades.

Romans 4:18–21 tells us:

“Against all hope, Abraham in hope believed…”

What does that mean?

Most of us would have been at the adoption agency decades before. We would have tackled the problem head-on. Abraham saw it differently:

Circumstances said "no"
Time said "no"
Logic said "no"

But Abraham said:

"God said yes."

And he stayed there.

The Bible says:

"He did not waver…"

That is faith that outlasts delay.

Not perfect faith.

Persistent faith.

Faith that refuses to move.

Even when everything else is shifting.

THE ENEMY ATTACKS FAITH OVER TIME

The enemy doesn't always try to destroy your faith immediately.

He tries to wear it down gradually through questions like:

- "Is this really going to happen?"
- "Did God really say that?"
- "How much longer can you keep believing?"

And if you're not careful...

Faith becomes:

- Weak
- Uncertain
- Conditional

We must be aware and keep our eyes on the prize. It does no good for anyone because we walk away too soon.

- "Faith doesn't usually collapse—it erodes."
- "Doubt grows where faith is not reinforced."
- "What you feed determines what survives."

SO HOW DO YOU SUSTAIN FAITH?

Faith that lasts is not accidental.

It is intentional.

1. You Anchor in the Word.

Faith is not based on feelings.

It is based on what God said.

Romans 10:17 offers us hope:

"Faith comes by hearing… and hearing by the Word of God."

If you lose the Word—you lose your foundation.

2. You Guard Your Mind.

Because faith and doubt both grow in the same place:

Your thoughts must remain centered on God.

Philippians 4:8 directs us:

"Think on these things…"

You cannot meditate on doubt…

And expect to live in faith.

3. You Stay Consistent.

Faith is not built in moments.

It is built in habits.

- Daily prayer
- Daily trust
- Daily obedience

Small consistency produces strong faith.

4. You Remember What God Has Done.

One of the greatest ways to sustain faith…

Is to remember.

Psalm 77:11 encourages us:

"I will remember the works of the Lord…"

If God did it before…

He can do it again.

DANIEL HAD HISTORY WITH GOD

By the time we see Daniel in chapter 10…

He already knew:

God is faithful
God responds
God moves

So he stayed in faith.

Even when nothing changed.

Faith is not about feeling strong.

Let me help someone here.

Faith is not:

Always feeling confident…
Always feeling certain…
Always feeling bold…

Faith is a decision.

A decision to believe:

Even when you don't feel it…
Even when you don't see it…
Even when you don't understand it…

- "Faith is not a feeling—it is a choice."
- "You don't have to feel strong to stand strong."
- "Faith is choosing God's Word over your situation."

THE POWER OF 'NEVERTHELESS' FAITH

One of the strongest forms of faith in Scripture is this:

"Nevertheless"

Habakkuk 3:17–18 assures us:

“Though the fig tree may not blossom…
Yet I will rejoice…”

That is mature faith.

Faith that says:

Even if nothing changes…
Even if nothing moves…

I still believe God.

That kind of faith cannot be broken.

Because it is not dependent on outcome.

It is rooted in God’s character.

FAITH THAT OUTLASTS DELAY PRODUCES BREAKTHROUGH

Let’s bring this back to Daniel.

Daniel prayed.

Nothing happened for 21 days.

But he didn’t quit.

And because he stayed…

The answer arrived.

What if he had stopped on day 20?

He would have missed…

What was already on the way.

And this happens more than we realize.

People quit:

Right before breakthrough…
Right before release…
Right before manifestation…

- "Don't quit one day before your answer arrives."
- "Breakthrough often comes to those who stay the longest."
- "If you hold on, you will see what God promised."

FINAL APPLICATION

Let me ask you:

Where is your faith being tested right now?

- In your waiting?
- In your prayers?
- In your promise?

And what would it look like…

To keep believing anyway?

CLOSING DECLARATION

Say this over your life:

- My faith will outlast the delay
- My belief will outlast the pressure
- My trust will outlast the silence
- And I will see what God promised

CLOSING THOUGHT

Faith that starts strong is good.

But faith that lasts…

Is powerful.

CLOSING PRAYER

Father,

Strengthen our faith.
Anchor us in Your Word.
Help us to believe… even when we don't see.

Give us the kind of faith…

That endures…
That stands…
That does not move…

Until we see everything You have promised.

In Jesus' name, Amen.

CHAPTER 9

HEAVEN IS WORKING ON YOUR BEHALF

One of the greatest lies the enemy will ever try to convince you of is this:

"Nothing is happening."

Because if he can get you to believe that…

He can get you to:

- Stop expecting
- Stop believing
- Stop standing

But nothing could be further from the truth.

Just because you don't see movement…

Does not mean there is no movement.

DANIEL REVEALS WHAT WE CANNOT SEE

In Daniel 10, we are given a glimpse behind the curtain of the natural world.

Daniel is praying.

Fasting.

Waiting.

And from his perspective…

Nothing is happening.

But heaven tells a different story.

The angel says:

"From the first day… your words were heard."

Which means:

> Heaven responded immediately.
> God moved instantly.
> The answer was already in motion.

Let that change your perspective.

While Daniel was waiting…

Heaven was working.

- “While you are waiting, heaven is working.”
- “God is never inactive—He is often unseen.”
- “Just because you don’t see movement doesn’t mean God isn’t moving.”

GOD IS ALWAYS MOVING BEHIND THE SCENES

One of the consistent patterns throughout Scripture is this:

God often works where you cannot see Him.

John 5:17 gives us this word:

Jesus said:

“My Father has been working until now…”

Notice that.

God is always working.

Even when it looks like nothing is happening.

Think about Joseph.

Joseph is in prison.

From the outside…

It looks like his life is stalled.

But behind the scenes:

- God is aligning people
- God is positioning Pharaoh
- God is orchestrating timing

And at the right moment…

Everything shifts.

This is how God works.

He moves:

- Quietly
- Strategically
- Intentionally

GOD IS NOT JUST WORKING—HE IS WORKING FOR YOU

Let's make this personal.

God is not just working in general.

He is working **on your behalf**.

Romans 8:28 tells us:

"All things work together for good…"

That means even what you don't understand...

God is using.

... even the delay

Even the resistance.

Even the waiting.

GOD IS WEAVING IT TOGETHER

For purpose.

For good.

For fulfillment.

- "God is not wasting your season—He is weaving it together."
- "What feels disconnected is being divinely orchestrated."
- "God is working in ways you cannot yet comprehend."

ANGELIC ACTIVITY IS REAL

Daniel 10 doesn't just show us delay...

It shows us activity.

The angel says:

> "I came because of your words…"
> "I was sent…"
> "I was resisted…"

That means heaven responds to earth.

Your prayers don't just disappear.

They activate movement.

Hebrews 1:14 tells us:

"Are they not all ministering spirits sent to serve…?"

Psalm 103:20 says:

"Angels… who do His word…"

Let this sink in.

When you pray…

Heaven moves.

You may not see it—but it is happening.

Angels are:

- Being dispatched
- Carrying out assignments

- Responding to God's command

Take it one more step by considering this:

- "Your prayers initiate movement in the unseen."
- "Heaven responds even when earth is silent."
- "You may not see it—but something is happening."

GOD IS ALSO ALIGNING TIMING

One of the most overlooked aspects of God's work…

Is timing.

Ecclesiastes 3:1 says:

"To everything there is a season…"

God is not just doing things—he is timing things.

Because the right thing…

At the wrong time…

Can become the wrong thing.

So God aligns everything.

- People
- Opportunities
- Circumstances
- Moments

And when it's right…

Everything comes together.

THIS IS WHY DELAY IS NECESSARY

Because timing matters.

- "God is not just preparing the promise—He is preparing the moment."
- "Timing is as important as the promise."
- "When God moves, everything aligns at once."

God is working in ways you don't expect.

Sometimes we expect God to move in obvious ways.

But often…

He is working in ways we would never anticipate.

Think about Esther.

She didn't see God moving.

There were no miracles recorded.

No supernatural events.

And yet—God was working.

- Positioning her
- Elevating her
- Placing her at the right moment

And at the right time…

Everything shifted.

God's work is not always loud.

Sometimes it is:

- Quiet
- Hidden
- Subtle

But it is always effective.

THE DANGER OF ASSUMING NOTHING IS HAPPENING

If you believe nothing is happening…

You will:

- Lose expectation

- Lose hope
- Lose faith

But when you know heaven is working…

You stay:

- Confident
- Anchored
- Expectant

FAITH CHANGES WHEN PERSPECTIVE CHANGES

When you understand that God is working…

You stop asking:

> "Is God doing anything?"

And you start declaring:

> "God is already at work."

FINAL APPLICATION

Let me ask you:

Where have you assumed nothing is happening?

- In your prayers?
- In your situation?

- In your waiting?

What if heaven is already moving?

What if:

- God has already responded
- The answer is already in motion
- Things are already shifting

What if you're closer than you think?

CLOSING DECLARATION

Say this over your life:

- Heaven is working on my behalf
- God is moving even when I don't see it
- My answer is already in motion
- And everything is coming together in His time

CLOSING THOUGHT

You are not waiting alone.

Heaven is engaged.

God is moving.

And what you cannot see…

Is already in progress.

CLOSING PRAYER

Father,

Thank You that You are always working.
Even when we don't see it…
Even when we don't feel it…

Help us to trust Your unseen activity.
Anchor us in Your promises.
And give us confidence…

That You are moving on our behalf.

In Jesus' name, Amen.

CHAPTER 10

YOU ARE NOT FIGHTING ALONE

There are moments in life when the battle feels personal.

The pressure feels targeted.
The struggle feels isolating.
The weight feels like it's yours to carry alone.

And if you're not careful…

You will begin to believe a dangerous lie:

"This is all on me."

THE ILLUSION OF ISOLATION

One of the enemy's greatest strategies…

Is to make you feel alone.

Because isolation weakens you.

It makes:

- Problems feel bigger
- *Pressure feel heavier*
- Hope feel smaller

But the truth is this:

You have never fought a battle alone.

DANIEL THOUGHT HE WAS JUST PRAYING

From Daniel's perspective, he was:

- Fasting
- Praying
- Waiting

That's all he could see.

But in the unseen realm…

There was:

- Movement
- *Conflict*
- Reinforcement

The angel tells him:

"I was sent because of your words..."
"I was resisted..."
"Michael came to help..."

Let that sink in.

While Daniel was praying...

Heaven was engaging.

- "You are not just praying—you are partnering."
- "What you do on earth activates what happens in heaven."
- "Your prayer life is not passive—it is powerful."

PRAYER IS NOT A MONOLOGUE—IT IS A PARTNERSHIP

Too often, we see prayer as:

Talking to God
Asking for help
Hoping something happens

But prayer is more than that.

Prayer is teamwork, holding hands with the Divine, and active participation in what God is doing.

WHEN YOU PRAY—HEAVEN RESPONDS

This is not symbolic.

This is real.

Jeremiah 33:3 assures us:

"Call to Me, and I will answer you…"

James 5:16 reinforces:

"The effective, fervent prayer of a righteous person avails much."

Your prayers matter more than you realize.

They are not empty words.

They are:

- Signals
- *Triggers*
- Activators

DANIEL'S WORDS MOVED HEAVEN

The angel didn't say:

> "I came because God decided…"

He said:

> "I came because of your words."

That means your prayers carry weight.

Angelic assistance is not fiction—it is biblical.

Let's address something clearly.

Daniel 10 shows us:

> Angels are real
>
> *Angels are active*
>
> Angels are involved

Hebrews 1:14 says:

"Are they not all ministering spirits sent to serve...?"

Psalm 34:7 tells us:

"The angel of the Lord encamps around those who fear Him..."

HEAVEN IS NOT PASSIVE

It is engaged.

You have help you cannot see.

Let that settle deep in your spirit:

There are things happening for you…

That you are completely unaware of.

- "Just because you can't see help doesn't mean help isn't present."
- "Heaven is more active in your life than you realize."
- "You are surrounded by what you cannot see."

Reinforcement comes when resistance increases.

In Daniel's situation…

The battle intensified.

And then—

Michael showed up.

That means this:

When resistance increased…

Reinforcement was released.

Let me say that again.

God does not leave you outmatched.

If the battle grows…

God sends more help to you.

Isaiah confirms this.

Isaiah 59:19

"When the enemy comes in like a flood…
the Spirit of the Lord lifts up a standard…"

YOU ARE NOT OUTNUMBERED

Even when it feels like it.

2 Kings 6 shows us this clearly.

Elisha's servant saw the enemy army.

He panicked.

But Elisha prayed:

"Lord, open his eyes…"

And when his eyes opened…

He saw:

More with them… than against them.

That is your reality too.

You may feel:

- Surrounded
- *Pressured*
- Outmatched

But the truth is that **you are supported**.

- "What is for you is greater than what is against you."
- "You are never outnumbered when heaven is involved."
- "The unseen support in your life outweighs the visible opposition."

JESUS PROMISED HIS PRESENCE

Let's bring this even closer.

Because beyond angels…

You have something greater.

Matthew 28:20 tells us:

"I am with you always…"

Hebrews 13:5 goes on to say:

"I will never leave you nor forsake you."

GOD HIMSELF IS WITH YOU

Not distant. Not removed.

Not watching from afar.

He is present:

In your:

- Battle
- *Waiting*
- Pressure
- *Process*

You are not carrying this alone.

This Changes Everything

When you realize you are not alone:

You don't:

- Panic
- *Retreat*
- Collapse

You stand:

With confidence.

With peace.

With strength.

Because you know:

God is with me
Heaven is helping me
I am not alone

FINAL APPLICATION

Let me ask you:

Where have you felt alone?

- In your struggle?
- In your waiting?
- In your battle?

What if you're not alone at all?

What if:

- Heaven is surrounding you
- God is strengthening you
- Help is already present

CLOSING DECLARATION

Say this over your life:

- I am not alone
- God is with me
- Heaven is helping me

- I have support I cannot see
- And I will stand in this battle

CLOSING THOUGHT

You may feel alone…

But you are not.

Heaven is engaged.

God is present.

And you are being supported…

In ways you cannot yet see.

CLOSING PRAYER

Father,

Thank You that we are never alone.
Thank You for Your presence, Your power, and Your help.

Open our eyes to see what we cannot see.
Strengthen us in the battle.
And remind us…

That You are always with us.

In Jesus' name, Amen.

CHAPTER 11

WHEN GOD SENDS REINFORCEMENTS

There are moments in life when what you're facing feels like too much.

Not just difficult…

But overwhelming.

The pressure increases.
The resistance intensifies.
The weight feels heavier than before.

And the question rises:

"Can I handle this?"

THE ANSWER IS—NOT ALONE

But here's the good news:

God never intended for you to handle it alone.

And more than that—

God knows exactly when to send reinforcement.

DANIEL'S BREAKING POINT

In Daniel 10, the angel reveals something powerful:

"The prince of Persia withstood me…
but Michael… came to help me…"

Don't miss this moment.

There was resistance.

There was delay.

There was conflict.

But then—help arrived.

Michael shows up.

Reinforcement is released.

And the battle shifts.

GOD SENDS HELP AT THE RIGHT TIME

Not too early.

Not too late.

Right on time.

- "God knows when the battle is too heavy for you alone."
- "Reinforcement is not random—it is strategic."
- "God never lets you face more than He is prepared to support."

Reinforcement comes when pressure peaks.

Have you ever noticed…

That things often get hardest…

Right before they shift?

That's not a coincidence.

That's a pattern.

In Exodus 14…

Israel is trapped:

- Red Sea in front
- Pharaoh behind

Pressure is at its highest point.

And that's when God moves.

The sea parts.

Not before the pressure.

At the peak of it.

Why?

Because God often allows the pressure…

To position you for the miracle.

- "God often waits until the pressure peaks before He parts the sea."
- "The moment you feel overwhelmed may be the moment God is about to move."
- "Your breaking point may be your breakthrough point."

GOD SEES WHAT YOU CANNOT SEE

One of the greatest comforts in Scripture is this:

God sees:

- The full picture
- *The full timeline*
- The full battle

You see the moment.

God sees the mission.

So when you feel overwhelmed…

God is not surprised.

He already has a plan.

And part of that plan includes:

Reinforcement

God sends what you need—when you need it.

Not always what you want.

But always what you need.

SOMETIMES REINFORCEMENT LOOKS LIKE STRENGTH

You don't get out of the situation…

But you get stronger in it.

Isaiah 40:29 tell us:

"He gives power to the weak..."

Sometimes it looks like people.

God sends:

- Encouragement
- *Support*
- Relationships

Sometimes it looks like clarity.

Suddenly you understand something you didn't before.

Sometimes it looks like...

... breakthrough.

And everything shifts.

But it always comes.

- "God's reinforcement may not look how you expect—but it always arrives."
- "God meets you at the point of your need."
- "Heaven never sends insufficient help."

Jesus modeled this in Gethsemane.

In **Luke 22:43**, it says:

"An angel appeared to Him from heaven, strengthening Him."

Think about that.

Jesus…

The Son of God…

Still received reinforcement.

If Jesus needed strengthening…

Why would we think we don't?

GOD STRENGTHENS YOU FOR WHAT YOU MUST WALK THROUGH

Notice:

Jesus wasn't removed from the cross.

He was strengthened for it.

That's important…

Because reinforcement doesn't always mean:

Escape.

Sometimes it means:

Endurance.

- "God doesn't always remove the pressure—He strengthens you in it."
- "Reinforcement is not always rescue—it is often empowerment."
- "God equips you for what He calls you to face."

YOU ARE NEVER LEFT UNSUPPORTED

Even when it feels like:

- No one understands
- *No one sees*
- No one is helping

Heaven is still engaged.

Psalm 121:1–2 says:

"I lift up my eyes…
My help comes from the Lord…"

That is your reality.

Your help…

Comes from God.

REINFORCEMENT CHANGES THE OUTCOME

Daniel's answer was delayed.

But when reinforcement came…

The breakthrough followed.

And that's what you need to understand.

You are not stuck.

You are not abandoned.

You are not forgotten.

Help is already assigned.

FINAL APPLICATION

Let me ask you:

Where does the pressure feel overwhelming right now?

- In your calling?
- In your family?
- In your faith?
- In your waiting?

What if reinforcement is already on the way?

What if:

- God has already seen it
- God has already responded
- God has already sent help

What if you're closer than you think?

CLOSING DECLARATION

Say this over your life:

- God is sending reinforcement
- I will not break under pressure
- I am being strengthened right now
- Help is on the way
- And I will make it through this

CLOSING THOUGHT

God knows the weight you're carrying.

And He knows exactly when to send what you need.

You will not be…

crushed.

You will be…

strengthened.

CLOSING PRAYER

Father,

Thank You that You never leave us unsupported.

Thank You that You send help at the right time.

Strengthen us where we feel weak.

Encourage us where we feel overwhelmed.

And remind us…

That You are always working on our behalf.

In Jesus' name, Amen.

CHAPTER 12

THE MOMENT EVERYTHING CHANGES

There comes a moment…

When everything shifts.

Not gradually.

Not slowly.

But suddenly.

After the waiting…

After the pressure…
After the resistance…
After the silence…

Something breaks open.

What felt stuck… moves.
What felt delayed… arrives.
What felt impossible… happens.

THE NATURE OF BREAKTHROUGH

Breakthrough rarely announces itself in advance.

It doesn't send a warning.

It doesn't give you a countdown.

It just happens.

Ecclesiastes 3:1 reminds us:

"To everything there is a season…"

And when the season changes—everything changes.

DANIEL'S MOMENT COMES

Daniel waited 21 days.

Nothing happened.

No sign.
No movement.
No response.

And, then—suddenly…

The angel appears.

The answer arrives.

The delay breaks.

And everything makes sense.

THE WAITING WAS NOT WASTED

The resistance was not final.

The silence was not empty.

It was all leading…

to this moment.

- "Breakthrough may be delayed—but it is never denied."
- "What takes time to arrive often comes suddenly."
- "God moves in moments that change everything."

SUDDENLY IS A BIBLICAL PATTERN

Throughout Scripture, breakthrough often comes suddenly.

Acts 2:2 says:

"Suddenly… there came a sound from heaven…"

Acts 16:26 says:

"Suddenly there was a great earthquake…"

Malachi 3:1 says:

"The Lord… will suddenly come…"

God moves in suddenlies…

Not because He was inactive…

But because He was preparing.

THE SUDDEN IS THE RESULT OF THE PROCESS

What you didn't see was building…

Was in full process behind the scenes.

- God was aligning
- *God was preparing*
- God was orchestrating

So, when it happens…

It feels immediate.

But it was always in motion.

- "Your suddenly is the result of unseen preparation."
- "What feels instant was actually in process."
- "God doesn't rush—but He does release."

BREAKTHROUGH FEELS DISPROPORTIONATE

Here's what's powerful:

Breakthrough often feels…

bigger than the struggle.

One moment changes everything.

One call.
One door.
One opportunity.
One answer.

And everything shifts.

This is how God works.

He can make up in a moment…

What took years to build.

Joel 2:25 tells us:

"I will restore the years…"

GOD REDEEMS TIME

Acceleration happens after delay.

What took a long time to arrive…

Can move quickly once it does.

Like a dam breaking…

Pressure builds.

Water collects.

And then suddenly—release.

- "Delay stores momentum—breakthrough releases it."
- "God can accelerate what seemed slow."
- "What was held back can suddenly be released."

WHY YOU MUST STAY READY

Here's the key:

When the moment comes…

You must be ready.

Because breakthrough requires response.

Daniel was still positioned.

He was:

- Still praying
- *Still seeking*
- Still aligned

So, when the answer came—he received it.

Many miss their moment…

Not because God didn't move…

But because they stopped believing.

They left too soon.

- "Breakthrough is received by those who remain positioned."
- "You don't just need faith to start—you need faith to stay."
- "Don't move out of position before God moves in your situation."

THE SHIFT CHANGES EVERYTHING

When God finally moves, when our answer

comes, ***when God gives us His release***, everything becomes new for us …

A replacement of the struggle and ***the answer that reaches us***:

- Clarity replaces confusion
- Peace replaces pressure
- Movement replaces stagnation

And suddenly…

Everything that felt unclear…

Becomes clear.

This is God's faithfulness.

He does not forget.

He does not abandon.

He does not fail.

Numbers 23:19 says:

"God is not a man, that He should lie…"

If He said it—He will do it.

FINAL APPLICATION

Let me ask you:

What are you believing for right now?

What feels:

- Delayed
- *Stuck*
- Unmoving

What if your suddenly is closer than you think?

What if:

- The answer is already near
- The shift is already coming
- The breakthrough is already set

What if everything is about to change?

CLOSING DECLARATION

Say this over your life:

- My moment is coming
- My season is shifting
- My breakthrough is near
- What was delayed is being released
- And everything is about to change

Then begin to live as though God's answer is already on the way.

Because it is!

CLOSING THOUGHT

You have waited.

You have endured.

You have stayed.

Now get ready…

Because when God moves…

Everything changes.

CLOSING PRAYER

Father,

Thank You for every promise You have spoken.
Thank You that You are faithful to fulfill.

Prepare us for the moment of breakthrough.
Position us to receive what You release.
And give us faith…

To believe that our moment is coming.

In Jesus' name, Amen.

CHAPTER 13

ACCELERATION AFTER DELAY

There is something powerful about how God works.

He does not just bring you out…

He brings you **forward**.

GOD DOESN'T JUST RESTORE—HE ACCELERATES

Many people think breakthrough simply means:

"Things are finally moving again"

But in the Kingdom of God…

Breakthrough often means:

Things begin to move faster than expected.

WHAT TOOK YEARS… CAN SHIFT IN MOMENTS

Because God is not limited by:

- Time
- *Process*
- Natural progression

God can do in a moment…

What would normally take years.

Joel 2:25 declares:

"I will restore to you the years…"

Let that settle in.

Not just moments.

Not just days.

Years.

GOD REDEEMS TIME

Time that felt:

- Lost
- *Wasted*
- Delayed

God can restore it.

- "God doesn't just restore what was lost—He redeems the time it took to lose it."
- "Delay is not the end of your story—it is the setup for acceleration."
- "God can make up for lost time in supernatural ways."

ACCELERATION IS A BIBLICAL PATTERN

Throughout Scripture, we see this repeated.

Joseph

He spent years in:

- The pit
- The prison

Then suddenly...

In one day:

He is elevated
He is promoted
He is positioned

From prison to palace.

That's acceleration.

David

After years of:

- Hiding
- *Running*
- Waiting

Then suddenly…

He becomes king.

The process was long.

The promotion was quick.

That's how God works.

Ecclesiastes 3:11 says:

"He makes everything beautiful in its time."

And when that time comes…

Things begin to align rapidly.

ACCELERATION FEELS LIKE EVERYTHING COMING TOGETHER

You start to notice:

- Doors open quickly

- Opportunities align
- Favor increases
- Momentum builds

What once felt slow…

Now feels fast.

- "God can move faster than your delay lasted."
- "Acceleration is the reward of endurance."
- "What took time to prepare can move quickly once released."

WHY ACCELERATION HAPPENS AFTER DELAY

Because delay was not empty.

It was:

- Preparation
- *Development*
- Alignment

So when release comes…

Everything is ready.

There is no more need to wait.

The dam has broken.

And momentum begins.

Amos 9:13 describes this powerfully:

"The plowman shall overtake the reaper…"

That means this:

Things begin to happen so quickly…

One season overlaps another.

Harvest comes while planting is still happening.

This is supernatural acceleration.

But here's the key: **you must be ready.**

Acceleration is powerful…

But it requires:

- Readiness
- *Capacity*
- Alignment

If you are not ready…

Acceleration can overwhelm you.

That's why development came first.

God prepared you…

Before He accelerated you.

- "God won't accelerate what you're not prepared to handle."
- "Preparation protects you in acceleration."
- "The waiting season was your training ground."

ACCELERATION REQUIRES STEWARDSHIP

When things begin to move quickly:

You must:

- Stay grounded
- *Stay focused*
- Stay dependent on God

Because speed can distract.

And blessing can become overwhelming…

If you lose alignment.

Stay anchored.

The same God who sustained you in the delay…

Must guide you in the acceleration.

ACCELERATION IS NOT JUST ABOUT YOU

Let's go deeper.

God doesn't accelerate just for your benefit.

He accelerates for impact.

Because what He's doing in your life…

Is connected to others.

Joseph's acceleration saved nations.

Your breakthrough carries purpose.

It's bigger than you.

- "God accelerates you so you can impact others."
- "Your breakthrough is connected to someone else's blessing."
- "What God does for you, He intends to do through you."

DON'T LET DELAY DEFINE YOU

Let me say this clearly:

Delay was a season.

Not your identity.

You Are Not 'behind'...

You are:

- Positioned
- *Prepared*
- Ready

And When God Moves...

You will not be behind.

You will be right on time.

FINAL APPLICATION

Let me ask you:

Where have you felt like you've lost time?

Where have you thought:

> "I'm behind..."
> "It's too late..."
> "I missed my moment..."

What if God is about to accelerate you?

What if:

- Time is being redeemed

- Opportunities are aligning
- Momentum is about to build

What if you're stepping into a season of acceleration?

CLOSING DECLARATION

Say this over your life:

- God is restoring my time
- God is accelerating my future
- What was delayed is being redeemed
- Momentum is building in my life
- And I am stepping into my season

CLOSING THOUGHT

Delay was not the end.

It was preparation.

And, now…

Acceleration is coming.

CLOSING PRAYER

Father,

Thank You that You redeem time.
Thank You that You restore what was lost.

Prepare us for acceleration.
Help us to steward what You release.
And align us with Your timing.

In Jesus' name, Amen.

CHAPTER 14

WHEN WHAT WAS HELD BACK IS RELEASED

There comes a moment in the life of every believer…

When what was delayed…

What was resisted…

What was held back…

Is finally released.

Not partially…

Not slowly...

Not incrementally...

But fully!

This is the moment you prayed for.

The moment you believed for.

The moment you held onto in the silence.

And when it happens…

It changes everything.

RELEASE FEELS DIFFERENT THAN DELAY

Delay feels:

- Heavy
- *Slow*
- Uncertain

But release feels:

- Clear
- *Certain*
- Immediate

The weight lifts.

The tension breaks.

The waiting ends.

And what was stuck… moves.

- “What was held back is not lost—it is reserved.”
- “God does not forget what He promised—He releases it at the right time.”
- “Delay stores what release reveals.”

DANIEL EXPERIENCED THIS SHIFT

For 21 days…

Nothing.

Then suddenly—

The answer arrives.

The resistance breaks.

The delay ends.

The message comes through.

And, everything changes.

This is the moment of release.

GOD DOES NOT RELEASE RANDOMLY

Let’s be clear:

Release is not accidental.

It is intentional.

God releases when:

- The timing is right
- *The person is ready*
- The alignment is complete

Because release carries responsibility.

- "God releases when readiness meets timing."
- "What God gives you, you must be ready to carry."
- "Release follows preparation."

RELEASE OFTEN COMES WITH OVERFLOW

God rarely just meets the need.

He exceeds it.

Ephesians 3:20 says:

"He is able to do exceedingly abundantly above all…"

That means this:

What God releases…

Is often greater than what you expected.

Because God doesn't just answer—He exceeds.

THINK ABOUT JOB

He lost everything.

But when God restored him…

He received double.

That's not recovery…

That's overflow.

THINK ABOUT THE PRODIGAL SON

He expected:

- Acceptance

But, received:

- Restoration
- *Celebration*
- Reinstatement

That's not just return.

That's release.

- “God doesn’t just restore—He multiplies.”
- “What God releases often exceeds what was lost.”
- “Overflow is God’s signature.”

RELEASE REQUIRES STEWARDSHIP

Let’s pause here…

Because this is important.

When God releases…

You must be ready to:

- Handle it
- *Carry it*
- Steward it

Because what you prayed for…

Now requires responsibility.

And if you’re not careful…

You can mishandle what you once waited for.

STAY GROUNDED

The same disciplines that sustained you in delay…

Must sustain you in release.

- Prayer
- *Dependence*
- Humility

It's vital that you don't allow yourself to drift…

- "Don't lose in release what you built in delay."
- "The same God who brought you through must keep you grounded."
- "Stewardship determines sustainability."

RELEASE BRINGS CLARITY

One of the most powerful things about release is this:

It makes everything make sense.

You look back and realize:

- Why it took time
- *Why it didn't happen earlier*
- Why you had to go through what you went through

The process becomes clear.

Romans 8:28 comes alive:

"All things work together…"

Not just some things.

All things.

Even the delay.

Even the struggle.

Even the waiting.

God used it all.

RELEASE ALSO BRINGS TESTIMONY

What God does in your life…

Is not just for you.

It becomes a testimony.

Revelation 12:11 says:

"They overcame… by the word of their testimony…"

Your story matters.

Because someone else is:

- In delay
- *In resistance*
- In waiting

And, your breakthrough becomes their hope.

- "Your breakthrough is someone else's encouragement."
- "What God brings you through becomes what He speaks through you."
- "Your testimony carries power."

DON'T FORGET GOD IN THE RELEASE

This is critical.

Sometimes when things finally happen…

People:

- Get busy
- *Get distracted*
- Move forward

And forget the One who brought them there.

Deuteronomy 8:10–11 warns us:

"Do not forget the Lord…"

Stay connected.

Because the blessing is not the goal—**God is**.

FINAL APPLICATION

Let me ask you:

What are you believing God to release?

What has felt:

- Held back
- *Delayed*
- Out of reach

What if it's not lost…

… just reserved?

What if:

- The timing is aligning
- *The preparation is complete*
- The release is near

What if everything is about to be released?

CLOSING DECLARATION

Say this over your life:

- What was held back is being released
- What was delayed is arriving
- What was resisted is breaking through
- And I am stepping into what God promised

CLOSING THOUGHT

What was held back…

Was never lost.

It was waiting…

For the right moment.

And, when that moment comes…

Everything is released.

CLOSING PRAYER

Father,

Thank You that You are faithful to release what You have promised.
Thank You that nothing You have spoken is lost.

Prepare us to receive.
Teach us to steward.
And help us to remain grounded in You.

In Jesus' name, Amen.

CHAPTER 15

LIVING ON THE OTHER SIDE OF DELAY

There is a side of faith we don't talk about enough.

We talk about:

- Believing
- *Waiting*
- Enduring
- *Breaking through*

But, what about after?

What happens when:

- The prayer is answered
- *The door opens*
- The promise is fulfilled

How do you live on the other side of delay?

BREAKTHROUGH IS NOT THE END

It's the beginning.

You prayed for it… now you must walk in it.

This is where many people struggle.

They know how to:

- Pray for the promise
- Believe for the promise

But they don't know how to live in it.

The transition can be challenging…

Because everything changes.

You go from:

- Waiting → Walking
- Hoping → Handling
- Believing → Bearing responsibility

And that requires maturity.

- "Breakthrough introduces you to a new level—maturity keeps you there."

- “Receiving is one thing—sustaining is another.”
- “What God gives you must now be stewarded.”

THE SAME GOD WHO BROUGHT YOU THROUGH MUST KEEP YOU THERE

Let’s be clear:

You did not arrive by your own strength.

And you cannot remain by your own strength.

Dependence must continue.

The same:

- Prayer
- *Faith*
- Humility

That carried you through delay…

Must carry you through fulfillment.

Deuteronomy 8 Warns:

When everything is going well…

There is a danger.

Deuteronomy 8:17–18 cautions us:

"Beware lest you say… my power… has gotten me this wealth…"

SUCCESS CAN CREATE SUBTLE PRIDE

You forget the process.

You forget:

- The waiting
- *The prayers*
- The dependence

And that's dangerous.

- "Never forget what it took to get where you are."
- "The same humility that got you there must keep you there."
- "If you disconnect from God in success, you weaken your future."

STAY GROUNDED

Living on the other side of delay requires:

- Stability
- *Confidence*
- Trust

Because everything is moving now.

Momentum is real.

Opportunities are increasing.

Responsibility is growing.

And if you're not grounded…

You can become overwhelmed.

STAY ROOTED IN GOD

John 15:5 says to:

"Abide in Me…"

Abiding is not optional.

It is essential.

Because fruit requires connection.

STEWARDSHIP IS THE KEY TO SUSTAINABILITY

Let's talk about stewardship.

Because what God gives…

Must be managed.

Luke 16:10 admonished us:

"He who is faithful in little…"

Faithfulness doesn't stop at breakthrough.

It becomes more important.

Now you must:

- Guard what God gave
- *Grow what God gave*
- Honor God with what He gave

Be aware that:

- "What you don't steward, you can lose."
- "Faithfulness sustains what favor releases."
- "God gives—but you must manage."

DON'T LET FULFILLMENT REPLACE HUNGER

This is critical.

Sometimes when the need is met…

The hunger fades.

But hunger is…

What keeps you growing.

Matthew 5:6 tells us:

“Blessed are those who hunger…”

Never lose your hunger for God…

Because the promise…

Is not the destination.

God is.

- “Don’t let what God gave you replace your pursuit of Him.”
- “Stay hungry—even when you are full.”
- “Your relationship with God must outlast your need for breakthrough.”

YOUR LIFE NOW CARRIES INFLUENCE

Let’s go deeper.

When God brings you through delay…

And into fulfillment…

Your life becomes:

A testimony.

People are watching.

They see:

- Your journey
- *Your breakthrough*
- Your outcome

And your life speaks.

Now you carry responsibility.

Not just to receive…

But to represent.

- “Your life is now evidence that God is faithful.”
- “What God did in you, He wants to display through you.”
- “You are living proof that delay is not denial.”

HELP OTHERS WHO ARE STILL WAITING

Never forget:

There are people still in the place you came from.

Encourage them.

Strengthen them.

Remind them: **"Don't quit."**

2 Corinthians 1:4 tells us:

"He comforts us… so we can comfort others…"

YOUR STORY HAS PURPOSE

Guard against complacency.

This is one of the greatest dangers after breakthrough.

Comfort can lead to complacency.

And, complacency leads to stagnation.

KEEP GROWING

Keep:

- Seeking
- *Learning*
- Pursuing

Because God is not finished.

FINAL APPLICATION

Let me ask you:

Now that God has brought you through something…

How are you living on the other side?

Are you:

- Still dependent?
- *Still hungry?*
- Still faithful?

Or, have you moved on from what sustained you?

CLOSING DECLARATION

Say this over your life:

- I will steward what God has given me
- I will remain dependent on God
- I will stay grounded and faithful
- I will not forget what God has done
- And I will live in the fullness of His promise

CLOSING THOUGHT

You made it through the delay.

You endured the process.

You saw the breakthrough.

Now live in it...

With wisdom.
With humility.
With faithfulness.

Because this is not the end…

It's the beginning of what God will do next.

CLOSING PRAYER

Father,

Thank You for bringing us through.
Thank You for every promise fulfilled.

Help us to steward what You've given.
Keep us humble.
Keep us hungry.
Keep us dependent on You.

And let our lives reflect Your faithfulness.

In Jesus' name, Amen.

CHAPTER 16

HOW TO SURVIVE THE SILENCE

There are seasons in your life…

When God feels quiet.

Not absent.

Not distant.

Just… quiet.

You pray…

And there's no response.

You believe…

And there's no movement.

You wait…

And nothing changes.

This is the silence.

And if you don't understand it…

It can become one of the most dangerous seasons of your life.

Because silence tests what noise cannot.

SILENCE IS WHERE FAITH IS PROVEN

Anyone can believe God when:

- Things are happening
- *Prayers are being answered*
- Breakthrough is visible

But what about when nothing is happening?

That's where faith becomes real.

Psalm 13:1 pleads:

"How long, O Lord… will You forget me forever?"

Even David experienced silence.

And yet—he stayed.

SILENCE IS NOT ABSENCE

Let's settle this immediately:

God's silence is not God's absence.

Isaiah 45:15 tells us:

"Truly, You are a God who hides Himself…"

God is still present.

Even when He is not speaking.

God is still working.

Even when you cannot see it.

- "Silence does not mean God is inactive—it means He is unseen."
- "God's quiet does not equal God's absence."
- "Just because God isn't speaking doesn't mean He isn't moving."

WHY DOES GOD ALLOW SILENCE?

This is the question everyone asks.

1. Silence Reveals What You Really Believe.

When God speaks…

Faith is easy.

But, when He is silent…

Your belief is tested.

Do you trust what He said…

Even when He's not saying anything new?

Because mature faith doesn't need constant reassurance.

2. Silence Deepens Dependence.

When everything is loud…

You rely on what you hear.

But, when it's quiet…

You learn to rely on:

- His character
- *His nature*
- His faithfulness

3. Silence Strengthens Your Spirit.

Noise can carry you.

But, silence builds you.

Because now you must stand…

Without feeling.

Without confirmation.

Without visible progress.

- "Silence forces your faith to stand on truth, not feelings."
- "God's quiet seasons produce strong believers."
- "When God is silent, He is strengthening you."

JESUS EXPERIENCED SILENCE TOO

On the cross, Jesus cried out.

Matthew 27:46 reveals His words:

"My God, My God… why have You forsaken Me?"

In that moment…

Heaven was silent.

But God was not absent.

What looked like silence…

Was actually the moment of greatest victory.

DON'T MISINTERPRET THE SILENCE

This is critical.

Silence can feel like:

- Rejection
- *Delay*
- Distance

But, it is not those things.

It is often:

- Preparation
- *Positioning*
- Process

If you misread silence…

You will:

- Pull back
- *Lose faith*
- Quit too soon

And if that happens:

- "If you misinterpret silence, you will mishandle the season."

- “God’s quiet is not rejection—it is preparation.”
- “Don’t walk away in a season where God is still working.”

HOW DO YOU SURVIVE THE SILENCE?

Let’s get practical.

1. Go Back to What God Already Said.

When God is not saying something new…

Hold onto what He already said.

Habakkuk 2:2–3 says:

“Write the vision… though it tarries… wait for it…”

God doesn’t change His Word.

2. Stay Consistent.

Don’t let silence change your discipline.

Keep:

- Praying
- *Reading*
- Trusting

Consistency sustains you in silence.

3. Guard Your Mind.

Silence creates space.

And, if you're not careful…

That space will be filled with:

- Doubt
- *Fear*
- Assumptions

Philippians 4:8 tells us:

"Think on these things…"

What you think matters.

4. Stay Connected to God.

Don't withdraw.

Lean in.

Because the answer to silence…

Is not distance.

It is…

… deeper connection.

5. Keep Expectation Alive.

Just because you don't see movement…

Doesn't mean movement isn't coming.

Expectation protects your faith.

- "Don't let silence silence your faith."
- "Consistency in silence leads to breakthrough in time."
- "Stay where God placed you—even when you don't hear Him."

Daniel survived the silence…

For 21 days…

He received nothing in answer.

But, he stayed.

And, because he stayed…

He saw the answer.

WHAT IF HE HAD QUIT EARLY?

He would have missed:

What was already on the way.

And this happens every day.

People quit:

- In the silence
- *In the waiting*
- In the unknown

Don't be one of them.

FINAL APPLICATION

Let me ask you:

Where is God silent in your life right now?

- In your prayers?
- *In your situation?*
- In your direction?

And what would it look like…

To stay anyway?

To trust anyway?

To believe anyway?

CLOSING DECLARATION

Say this over your life:

- God is with me—even in the silence
- God is working—even when I don't see it

- I will not quit in a quiet season
- I will trust what God has already said
- And I will stay until breakthrough comes

CLOSING THOUGHT

Silence is not the end.

It is the space…

Where faith is built.

And if you survive the silence…

You will see the breakthrough.

CLOSING PRAYER

Father,

Help us to trust You in the silence.
Strengthen us when we don't hear You.
Anchor us in what You have already spoken.

Give us the faith to stay…
The strength to endure…
And the confidence to believe…

That You are working—even now.

In Jesus' name, Amen.

CHAPTER 17

STANDING STRONG IN SPIRITUAL WATERS

By now, you understand something clearly:

- Delay is real
- *Resistance is real*
- Weariness is real
- *Silence is real*

But, so is victory.

The question is no longer:

"Is there a battle?"

The question is:

"How do I stand in it?"

Because the goal is not just to fight.

The goal is to:

> **Stand... and remain standing.**

EPHESIANS GIVES US THE BLUEPRINT

In **Ephesians 6:13**, Paul says:

"Having done all… to stand."

That's powerful!

Not run.
Not retreat.
Not collapse.

Stand.

STANDING IS A POSITION OF STRENGTH

Standing means:

> You're still here.
> *You're still believing.*
> You haven't moved.

And, that alone is victory.

- “Victory is not always loud—sometimes it is simply standing.”
- “You don’t have to win quickly—you just have to not quit.”
- “Standing is a spiritual act of defiance.”

Spiritual warfare is not always what you think.

Many people imagine spiritual warfare as dramatic.

But, often… it’s simple.

It looks like:

- Choosing faith over doubt
- *Choosing prayer over silence*
- Choosing obedience over compromise

The battle is in your daily decisions.

THE BATTLEFIELD IS YOUR MIND

Let’s go deeper.

2 Corinthians 10:4–5 says:

“We cast down arguments…
and every thought…”

The real war happens in your thinking.

Because what you believe…

Determines how you live.

If the enemy can influence your thoughts…

He can weaken your faith.

So, you must guard your mind.

Romans 12:2 instructs us:

“Be transformed by the renewing of your mind…”

You don’t win the battle externally…

If you lose it internally.

- “The battle you ignore in your mind will show up in your life.”
- “Your thoughts are the front line of your faith.”
- “Win your mind—and you strengthen your life.”

YOU MUST PUT ON THE ARMOR

Ephesians 6 doesn’t just tell us to stand.

It tells us how.

Ephesians 6:14–17 describes the:

- Belt of truth
- Breastplate of righteousness
- Shield of faith
- Helmet of salvation
- Sword of the Spirit

This is not symbolic—it's practical.

Truth anchors you.

Without truth…

You become unstable.

Righteousness protects you.

When you walk in integrity…

You remove openings for the enemy.

Faith shields you.

Faith blocks:

- Doubt
- *Fear*
- Lies

Salvation covers your mind.

You remember who you are.

The Word becomes your weapon.

You don't just defend…

You fight back.

Jesus modeled this.

When tempted in the wilderness…

Jesus responded with:

"It is written…"

That's how you fight.

- "You don't fight the enemy with emotion—you fight with truth."
- "The Word is not just information—it is a weapon."
- "When you speak the Word, you shift the battle."

PRAYER IS YOUR POWER

Let's not miss this.

Ephesians 6:18 says:

"Praying always…"

Prayer is not optional in warfare.

It is essential.

Because prayer keeps you connected.

And connection gives you strength.

Daniel's victory was rooted in prayer.

He didn't fight physically.

He fought spiritually.

And, heaven responded.

YOU MUST STAY CONSISTENT

Victory is not built in moments.

It is built in consistency.

Daily choices matter.

- Daily faith
- *Daily prayer*
- Daily obedience

Because the battle is ongoing.

- "Consistency wins battles that intensity cannot sustain."
- "You don't need a moment—you need a lifestyle."
- "Victory is built daily, not occasionally."

YOU ARE ALREADY EQUIPPED

Let me remind you:

You are not trying to get victory.

You already have it.

Romans 8:37 assures you:

"We are more than conquerors…"

You are not fighting ***for victory*.**

You are fighting ***from victory*.**

That changes everything.

You don't fight in fear.

You stand in confidence.

You don't fight uncertain.

You stand assured.

Because God is with you.

FINAL APPLICATION

Let me ask you:

Where is the battle in your life right now?

- In your mind?
- In your faith?
- In your situation?

And, how are you responding?

Are you:

- Standing…
- Or retreating?

What would it look like…

To stand today?

CLOSING DECLARATION

Say this over your life:

- I will stand in this battle
- I will not be moved by pressure
- I will guard my mind
- I will stand on God's Word
- And I will walk in victory

CLOSING THOUGHT

The battle is real.

But so is your strength.

And, if you stand…

You will see victory.

CLOSING PRAYER

Father,

Strengthen us for the battle.
Help us to stand firm in faith.
Guard our minds, anchor our hearts, and steady our steps.

Teach us to fight with truth…
To stand with confidence…
And to trust that victory is already ours.

In Jesus' name, Amen.

CHAPTER 18

DELAYED... BUT NEVER DENIED

There is a phrase that has echoed through every chapter of this journey:

Delayed... but not denied.

Now it's time to understand it fully.

Because this is not just a statement...

It is a revelation.

DELAY HAS A PURPOSE

Delay is not random.

It is not careless.

It is not God forgetting.

Delay is intentional.

It is where:

- Faith is tested
- Character is developed
- Capacity is increased
- Trust is deepened

Everything you walked through…

… mattered.

Nothing was wasted.

Not the waiting.
Not the struggle.
Not the silence.

God used it all.

Romans 8:28 reminds us:

"All things work together…"

Even the parts you didn't understand.

- "Delay is not denial—it is development."
- "God never wastes a season—He works in it."
- "Everything you went through prepared you for what you're walking into."

DENIAL WOULD MEAN IT'S OVER

Let's define the difference.

Denial means:

- It's canceled
- It's finished
- It's not going to happen

But, delay means:

- It's coming
- It's in process
- It's still on the way

THAT'S THE KEY

If God spoke it…

It is not denied.

Numbers 23:19 describes God:

"God is not a man, that He should lie…"

If He said it—He will do it.

YOU DIDN'T MISHEAR GOD

Let me speak to someone directly:

You didn't imagine it.

You didn't make it up.

God spoke to you.

And just because it hasn't happened yet…

Doesn't mean it won't.

It means it's still in process.

- "God's promises don't expire—they unfold."
- "Just because it hasn't happened doesn't mean it won't."
- "Delay is the process of promise becoming reality."

THE ENEMY WANTS YOU TO MISLABEL DELAY

If he can convince you that delay is denial…

You will walk away.

You will:

- Stop believing
- *Stop expecting*
- Stop standing

And, miss what was coming.

BUT, NOW YOU KNOW

Delay:

- Has purpose
- *Has process*
- Has timing

And it leads to fulfillment.

YOU MADE IT THROUGH

Let's pause and recognize something.

You didn't quit.

You:

- Stayed in faith
- *Stayed in prayer*
- Stayed in position

And, that matters…

Because many don't.

But you did…

And that means you're ready.

Ready for:

- The promise

- *The responsibility*
- The next season

This is what God wants you to hear:

- "Endurance qualifies you for what God promised."
- "You didn't survive the delay for nothing."
- "You are ready for what God is about to release."

YOUR STORY IS NOT FINISHED

Let me remind you:

This is not the end.

It's a transition.

From:

- Waiting → Walking
- Believing → Receiving
- Praying → Possessing

GOD STILL HAS MORE

Philippians 1:6 is our reason to rejoice:

"He who began a good work… will complete it…"

God finishes what He starts.

Live with expectation…

From this point forward.

You don't live:

- Wondering
- *Doubting*
- Questioning

You live expecting God's answers to your needs.

Because now you know:

God is working.
Heaven is moving.
The answer is coming.

- "Expectation is the posture of faith."
- "Live like God is about to move."
- "What you expect shapes how you stand."

You will see it.

Not maybe.

Not possibly.

You will see it unconditionally and in good time.

Psalm 27:13 is our promise:

"I would have lost heart… unless I had believed…"

That's the difference.

Belief kept you.

And, belief will carry you.

FINAL APPLICATION

Let me ask you one final question:

What in your life still feels delayed?

And, what would change…

If you truly believed…

… that it is not denied?

How would you:

- Pray differently?
- *Think differently?*
- Stand differently?

Because everything shifts when you understand this truth.

CLOSING DECLARATION

Say this with conviction:

- What God promised is still coming
- What God spoke is still true
- What feels delayed is not denied
- I will not quit
- I will not step back
- I will stand until I see it

FINAL THOUGHT

Delay was never your defeat.

It was your development

And, now…

You stand on the other side with this truth:

Delayed… But Never Denied

FINAL PRAYER

Father,

Thank You for every promise You have spoken.
Thank You that You are faithful to fulfill.

Seal this truth in our hearts:
That delay is not denial.

Strengthen us to stand.
Anchor us in faith.
And lead us into everything You have prepared.

And we declare it done—

In the mighty, marvelous, majestic, and matchless name of JESUS,

Amen.

A FINAL WORD

You can find Tim on the South Texas District website at www.stxag.org, on Facebook, or at his Houston office when he's not traveling his home state ministering in the churches across the South Texas District.

He'd be thrilled to connect with you and share stories of God's faithfulness.

www.ingramcontent.com/pod-product-compliance
Lightning Source LLC
LaVergne TN
LVHW020713110826
845149LV00012B/2245

* 9 7 9 8 9 9 5 9 5 7 7 0 6 *